EVAN
CAl

Why the Doctrines of Grace Are Good News

John Benton

THE BANNER OF TRUTH TRUST

THE BANNER OF TRUTH TRUST
3 Murrayfield Road, Edinburgh EH12 6EL, UK
PO Box 621, Carlisle, PA 17013, USA

*

ISBN-10: 0 85151 929 6
ISBN-13: 978 0 85151 929 6

*

Typeset in 10.5/12.5 pt Adobe Garamond
at the Banner of Truth Trust
Printed in the USA by
VersaPress, Inc.,
East Peoria, IL.

EVANGELISTIC CALVINISM

Why the Doctrines of Grace Are Good News

There are at least two vital elements in true gospel preaching. One is obviously telling people the facts about Jesus Christ and his atoning work. The second builds on the first; having announced the facts, we must then use them as the basis to persuade men and women to come to the Lord Jesus Christ for salvation. These two elements are to be found in the examples of apostolic preaching that we find in the New Testament. Gospel truth has within it the grounds for exhorting 'all people everywhere to repent'[1] and trust in the Saviour.

Of Peter on the day of Pentecost Luke tells us, 'With many other words he *warned* them; and he *pleaded* with them, "Save yourselves from this corrupt generation."'[2] The apostle Paul describes his own evangelistic ministry in similar terms: 'Since we know what it is to fear the Lord, we try to *persuade* men', and goes on to say, 'We therefore are Christ's ambassadors, as though God were making his appeal through us. We *implore* you on Christ's behalf: Be reconciled to God.'[3]

In the years 1618-19 a gathering of godly church leaders met in Holland, in what has become known as the Synod of Dort. Confronted with the teachings of Jacob Arminius, which they recognized to be a defection from the Bible's teaching on the subject of God's grace, they drew up from Scripture five counter-points of doctrine. These Bible truths are popularly known as 'the five points of Calvinism' and are summarized by the well-known acronym T-U-L-I-P.

It would of course be wrong to give the impression that the 'glorious gospel of the blessed God' can be reduced to these five stark points of doctrine. Looked at from one angle, the five points of Calvinism try to do the impossible by supplying us with a handy, thumbnail sketch – a synopsis – of God's great plan of salvation for

[1] *Acts* 17:30.　[2] *Acts* 2:40.　[3] 2 *Cor.* 5:11, 20.

a lost world. But can we really sum up, in such short compass, the wonderful works of our infinite and mysterious sovereign God whose 'greatness no one can fathom'?[4] Who can fully appreciate the enormity of our sin against the Almighty or comprehend all the details involved in God's plan to rescue sinners? Any study of the doctrines of grace ought to be placed within the context of a full Trinitarian theology, making a careful note of all the necessary balances, nuances, and depths of profundity. However, while summaries and synopses have their limitations, they can also be immensely useful. How many of us, for example, without a full Road Atlas, have nevertheless found our way to our destination with the help of a sketch-map drawn by a friend? Without that simple sketch-map we would have got totally lost! The five points of Calvinism are a very useful hand-drawn theological sketch-map. Yes, they may be better understood in the context of larger theological considerations; but they summarize vital truth and keep us on course in the work of the gospel. We should be very grateful that the theologians of Dort were so anxious to safeguard the gracious character of gospel salvation as to draw up these five points, and that many, if not all, of the great Reformed confessions of faith give expression, in some way or other, to these glorious 'doctrines of grace'.

What do these doctrines teach? Well, 'Total Depravity', the first truth signified by the T-U-L-I-P acronym, refers to the spiritual condition of mankind lost in sin. Then, with regard to God's sovereign decree of salvation, the second point is 'Unconditional Election'. In the next place, the Synod of Dort taught what is sometimes called 'Limited Atonement' with reference to the death of Christ. Fourthly, concerning how sinners come to faith in Christ, the Dutch divines understood the Scriptures to declare the truth of 'Irresistible Grace'. And fifthly, the Synod maintained that those who truly belong to Jesus Christ never finally fall away from grace, but are kept in the faith and enabled to keep trusting the Saviour to the end of their earthly lives. This last doctrine is usually referred to as the 'Perseverance of the Saints'.

4 *Psa.* 145:3.

Sadly, these five Bible truths are not only ignored and despised by the world but are often considered unfashionable within the church of Jesus Christ. On not a few occasions preachers have misrepresented them as being narrow, harsh, and ungenerous doctrines; sometimes they have been denounced by those who see them as hindering the proclamation of the love of Christ to a dying world and as a stumbling block that prevents sinners being saved. Even those who are favourably disposed to Reformed theology sometimes feel a little embarrassed by these truths and anxious that they might somehow adversely affect their evangelistic endeavours.

But I want to argue that the very opposite ought to be the case. The doctrines of grace are in fact five beautiful diamonds from which the glories of Jesus wonderfully shine to attract those who are lost in sin. They address the sinner's deepest fears in the most heart-warming way imaginable. Rather than being truths of which we are to be wary, they are in fact an integral part of the gospel to be proclaimed.

In saying this, I do not want to imply that my fellow-believers, who may hold to Arminian doctrinal views, never preach the gospel; but I am saying that Arminianism, as a system of doctrine, is a distortion of the Bible's teaching on grace. The doctrines of grace, expressed in the five points of Calvinism, not only most clearly represent the truth of the gospel, they provide an excellent platform from which the gospel can be preached to the needy in all its wonderful glory. Within these five points are powerful and moving arguments with which to *'persuade* men' to look away from themselves to Jesus Christ for salvation. These truths display the heart of God's love and direct us to the One who is truly 'the friend of sinners'.[5] They are full of the same spiritual pulling power which drew sinners to Jesus Christ long ago during the days of his earthly ministry, when 'the tax-collectors and sinners were all gathering round to hear him'.[6]

So let us consider how the five points of Calvinism are good news for lost men and women. As we do so, please remember that these

[5] *Matt.* 11:19.   [6] *Luke* 15:1.

pages do not pretend to be a thorough defence of the doctrines of grace; for that you must look elsewhere. Neither are they a philosophical investigation into these truths. Not every question will be, or indeed can be, answered. Rather, my purpose is to encourage readers to see how these great truths can be extremely useful in our preaching of the gospel, as we 'persuade', 'plead with', and 'implore' sinners to be reconciled to God.

How then, are the five points helpful to the Christian in the work of evangelism? Let us consider each of the truths in turn.

TOTAL DEPRAVITY

In the phrase 'total depravity' we have a description of the spiritual condition of every member of the human race. The word 'depravity' refers to something that is bad in character. This doctrine teaches us that we are not merely ignorant people who merely need to learn a few lessons or who need to develop new spiritual techniques for tuning-in to God. Human nature is fallen from what God originally made it to be. We have become sinful, selfish, rebellious, and morally corrupt. We stand before a *holy* God who rightly exercises a zero tolerance towards sin.

Perhaps the term 'total depravity' is not the best way of expressing this doctrine for, at first sight, it may lead some to believe that all human beings are as wicked as they possibly can be. But the doctrine of total depravity does not teach such a thing. Rather, it shows us how every aspect of our humanity has been affected and vitiated by Adam's fall into sin. Sin has polluted and corrupted every part of us; every human faculty bears sin's ugly imprint.

In his letter to the Ephesians Paul reminds them of what they were before God's grace saved them:

> As for you, you were dead in your transgressions and sins, in which you used to live when you followed the ways of this world and of the ruler of the kingdom of the air, the spirit who is now at work in those who are disobedient. All of us

also lived among them at one time, gratifying the cravings of our sinful nature and following its desires and thoughts. Like the rest, we were by nature objects of wrath.[7]

Sin has not only stirred God's anger and wrath; it has also enslaved the whole of humanity. We live to 'gratify' self, but the self we gratify is in subjugation to sin. Without Christ 'we live' in the ways of the world, as with a habit which we neither can nor desire to break. Satan, 'the ruler of the kingdom of the air' is 'at work' in men, women, and children, thus ensuring their continued disobedience to God. Moreover, this enslavement to sin relates to all our inner faculties. Our minds are ensnared, and so we follow the 'thoughts' of our sinful nature. Our affections and feelings are corrupted with the 'desires' of the sinful nature. Our will is also enthralled so that we choose to 'follow' the ways of the world. Of course, it is not surprising that many do not acknowledge this description as being true of themselves. Only the Holy Spirit, by means of God's law, can bring a deep conscious awareness of sin home to the sinner. But the reality is that like poison dissolved in a glass of water, sin has permeated every part of the human personality – mind, heart, and will. Sin's contamination of every human being is total.

The consequence of humanity's fall into sin is that we are all spiritually dead towards God. Sin not only cuts us off from God, but it also makes it impossible for us (apart from God's grace and enabling) to make, or even want to make, any move towards God.

The Bible's teaching about human sin has never been popular and it is certainly not popular today. In fact our modern liberal society hates the very idea that we all belong to a fallen and condemned race. It seems that the one great aim of today's pop psychology is to flatter folk and make them feel good about themselves. It tells them how misunderstood they have been, and that they are wonderfully good people at heart. The whole focus is on one's self-esteem and how best to boost it. But the Bible's message is very different. It tells us that we are all sinful at heart, that our

[7] *Eph.* 2:1-3.

character is basically bad, that we are lost, and that we are impotent to rescue ourselves from our plight.

How then can the doctrine of total depravity be good news? We might wonder what kind of crazy logic could ever turn this doctrine into a piece of encouraging news? But the fact is that this truth is surprisingly helpful to sinners for at least three reasons.

First it is good news because *this truth faces reality*. It tells us the truth about us and lets us know what we are really like. Yes, people may not be as evil as they might possibly be, and many do what we all recognize to be acts of goodness and kindness. But, nevertheless, we are all in rebellion against God and his laws, and the truth about our human nature is that which we see illustrated in our daily newspapers. The headlines confront us with political scandals, sexual immorality, and financial cover-ups. With sickening regularity the news tells us of yet another suicide bomb attack or another shooting incident at a school. Wives cheat on their husbands, and husbands cheat on their wives. Rich nations exploit their poorer neighbours. The Internet carries the evil of all kinds of wretched pornography. People are murdered, lies are told, and frauds are committed. The list goes on and is endless. The history of the human race is littered with atrocities of many kinds. The stark evidence reveals that there is no depth of wickedness to which human beings will not stoop. Modern western societies, which never seem to tire of telling us that human beings are not too bad, are frequently shocked and disappointed when faced with evidence to the contrary. But the truth of total depravity puts us in touch with the world as it really is. It shows us where we are actually located on the spiritual map. We now know where we are before God. In that sense it is good news.

But secondly, this doctrine is good news because *it provides us with the background for God's grace*. To our astonishment we discover that God loves sinners – people who are totally depraved! Since the Fall, we naturally imagine that there needs to be some goodness in us in order for God to be good and kind to us. But the gospel's breathtaking truth is that the love of God reaches out to people in whom, according to his own assessment, there is not one iota of pure goodness. Having outlined the nature of our sinful depravity to the Ephesian Christians, the apostle Paul adds, 'But because of his great love for us, God, who is rich in mercy, made us alive with Christ even when we were dead in transgressions.' No wonder he goes on to say, 'It is by grace you have been saved.'[8] Good news this most definitely is! If God loves those who can only be described as 'totally depraved' then no sinner is without hope; no one can be 'too bad' to be saved.

Thirdly, though this truth of total depravity humbles us, it also leads on to the further good news that *we can be transparently honest about ourselves before God.* There is no need to pretend that we are better than we really are. The good news is that God loves sinners – people with a bad character. His love extends even to those who see themselves as total failures and who hate themselves for what they are and have done. Because the Bible proclaims the good news about a God who loves real sinners, we can take off our masks and self-deceptions, and deal honestly with ourselves before God. This discovery is spiritual dynamite for every soul enslaved in sin.

One humorous quip asks: 'What is the difference between an optimist and a pessimist?' The answer given is, 'The optimist hasn't seen all the facts yet!' But the doctrine of total depravity makes us see all the worst facts about mankind in general and ourselves in particular, and, at the same time, holds out to us a great gospel hope. Surely this is something with which the Christian can warm the hearts of his unbelieving neighbours. It is good news.

UNCONDITIONAL ELECTION

We have already made mention of the love of God to depraved sinners, which alone brings salvation. But what is the origin of this love?

Turning again to his letter to the Ephesians, we see the apostle Paul providing the answer to this question.

[8] *Eph.* 2:4–5.

Praise be to the God and Father of our Lord Jesus Christ, who has blessed us in the heavenly realms with every spiritual blessing in Christ. For he chose us in him before the creation of the world to be holy and blameless in his sight. In love he predestined us to be adopted as his sons through Jesus Christ, in accordance with his pleasure and will – to the praise of his glorious grace which he has freely given us in the One he loves. In him we have redemption through his blood, the forgiveness of sins, in accordance with the riches of God's grace.[9]

In a democratic election with which we are familiar, the people choose a candidate to represent them; but here we are told that in love God chose these sinful people, in Ephesus and elsewhere, before the world was made. 'He chose us in him . . . In love he predestined us . . . ' God's choosing of sinners in eternity past Reformed theology calls 'unconditional election'. Yes, of course, when people become Christians they exercise their will and choose God. But what was it that led them to this strange and unusual course of action? According to the New Testament the sinner chooses God because God first chose them. This, of course, logically follows on from what we have just considered concerning total depravity. As sinners we were 'dead in transgressions and sins'. Left to ourselves we do not have the inclination or ability to move in a God-ward direction. If we are to do so, then God must take the initiative and make us both willing and able to do what is contrary to our own fallen nature. This merciful initiative of God is to be traced back to his decree of unconditional election.

However, we ought to sound a note of caution here because surrounding God's decrees there is an element of profound mystery. The Almighty is far greater than we his creatures can ever comprehend. We are finite and can never fathom the conundrum of how the sovereign purposes of the Almighty relate to the very personal decisions we make in this life. We know that we are not robots; conscience (as well as Scripture) bears witness that we are respons-

[9] *Eph.* 1:1-3.

ible for the choices we make. We choose freely, albeit in accordance with our nature. Yet when we respond to the gospel and freely come to Christ it can only be because God 'chose [us] to be saved through the sanctifying work of the Spirit and belief in the truth'.[10]

This is an awesome truth. Sadly there are some people who find it very disturbing because it declares that God is the One who is firmly in control. We like to see ourselves as the masters of our own destiny. But the Bible destroys human pride by proclaiming the sovereignty of God.

Yet can we not see how this uncomfortable doctrine can be used to overcome what is often the unspoken fear of many who hear the gospel? They listen to the message about Jesus dying for sinners and the call to turn from sin and receive Christ as Saviour. But in many there is a fear that, should they turn to Christ, God will not be kind to them. Well aware of their own sinfulness and unable to grasp the immensity of God's love to sinners, they seriously doubt a warm reception if they were to come to the Saviour. The best they could hope for would be some kind of grudging toleration. And Satan, the enemy of our souls, often uses such thoughts to keep many people like them outside the gates of God's kingdom.

But the doctrine of election *slays such fears and doubts once and for all.* Should we feel ourselves being drawn to Christ, this is ultimately God's doing. If we seek the Lord Jesus it must be because he deliberately sought us. Jesus said, 'All that the Father gives me will come to me and whoever comes to me I will never drive away.' Furthermore, he went on to say, 'No-one can come to me unless the Father who sent me draws him.'[11]

If sinners make their way to Jesus Christ they will soon discover the warmest of welcomes. They are being 'drawn' to Christ by the Father. Far from being gatecrashers at the party of God's salvation they are nothing less than 'A-list guests' of his own choosing. Therefore with such a cast-iron guarantee of God's welcome the doctrine of unconditional election urges sinners to come to Christ.

[10] *2 Thess.* 2:13.   [11] *John* 6:37, 44.

But this truth of God's choice goes further. It tells us that God's election is *unconditional*. In the words of Paul quoted above, this grace and salvation God 'has given us *freely* in the One he loves'. Sinners are not chosen on account of some merit, goodness, or ability that is to be found in them. Neither are they chosen because God saw beforehand that they would do something that would deserve his goodness. Such an idea denies the freeness of God's salvation – a freeness which the apostle speaks about here and elsewhere in his letters. God's grace is absolutely free. 'God saved us and called us to a holy life – *not because of anything we have done* but because of his own purpose and grace. This grace was given us in Christ Jesus before the beginning of time.'[12] Grace comes to us in Christ Jesus, and the only reason for this grace of election is God's own pleasure and will; it has nothing whatsoever to do with our fulfilling certain conditions. His grace is free. His is an unconstrained, sovereign, and unconditional choice.

Once again this is such a liberating truth to set before unconverted people. When approached with the gospel many people respond by saying, 'Sorry, but I'm not the type.' Some might even say to themselves: 'I would love to know that I am forgiven and will go to heaven when I die, but I know myself too well, and I'm just not the religious sort.' But this wonderful doctrine of unconditional election loudly declares that there is no 'type' that God chooses. In fact, God has chosen all 'sorts' – conditions do not apply!

I have sometimes wondered why the truth of election is so prominent in Paul's letter to the Ephesians. Although I cannot be sure, perhaps part of the answer lies in the kind of city Ephesus was. The Acts of the Apostles records how Paul brought the gospel to this great city in the Roman province of Asia Minor. Idolatry and magic of various kinds were to be found there.[13] The ancient Ephesians loved their astrology and horoscopes. They believed that the positions of the planets at the time of one's birth determine the kind of person one will be and the events that will take place in one's life.

[12] *2 Tim.* 1:8-9.   [13] *Acts* 19:9.

People were therefore categorized into various types: 'I'm a Sagittarian; you're a Gemini', etc. Even today people do the same kind of thing, not only in connection with astrology, but also with psychological testing. We are divided into various groupings: introverts and extroverts, or sensate and intuitive. Myers-Briggs personality tests might categorize you as ESTJ or INFP and so on. Don't we all tend to make assessments about other people's personalities? 'He's a bit of a loner', or 'She's just a good-time girl', we say. As a result of such thinking we tend to see ourselves as falling into one of these categories, and we may well conclude, 'I'm the wrong type for God.'

But unconditional election puts such thinking to the sword. God does not choose a certain type of person to save and transform into a Christian. God's choice is free. The witness of Scripture is that he has chosen all types, from sensuous party-going Samson to cunning, lying Jacob, and from beautiful, gentle Esther to the murderous religious bigot, Saul of Tarsus. He has chosen poor and rich, respectable citizens and despicable criminals, heterosexuals and homosexuals, all as objects of his transforming grace.[14] There are no age, class, gender, or racial limits. The Bible specifically informs us that he has chosen people from every language, tribe, and nation to be the heirs of his salvation. There are no restrictions to free grace.

We can therefore say to sinners, 'If God has chosen all types, then why not you?' Since their argument, 'I'm not the right type', holds no water, what leads them to be so sure that God has not chosen them? Besides, how do we know whom God has chosen? Can we know by simply looking at other people? No. Before conversion takes place the elect have no distinguishing marks. They are sinners and they do the things that sinners do. This is one good reason why the preacher must address the gospel to everyone in his congregation and the evangelist must offer Christ to all. 'How do I know if I am one of those God has chosen?' a sinner might be tempted to ask. They too will never know the answer to that question by

14 cf. *1 Cor.* 6:9–11.

looking at themselves in the mirror. They will only know by how they respond to the gospel's call: 'Will you have Jesus Christ to be your Lord and Saviour?' Should their response be a sincere 'Yes', then God is at work to save. Such a positive reaction, resulting in an ongoing commitment and an increasingly Christlike life, will make it evident to all that God has chosen them.

Once again, in this doctrine we find a certain, irresistible logic that urges people not to hesitate, but to come to Christ immediately. When properly understood and sympathetically proclaimed, the doctrines of grace knock down every barrier in order to bring sinners to Christ. It is tragic when those who oppose the doctrines of grace misrepresent them as part of an outdated and evangelistically inept theology. These doctrines form part of God's glorious truth and ought to be shouted with joy from the rooftops. These truths underline the fact that whoever needs to be saved, whatever they have done, may come, just as they are, to Jesus Christ.

Having looked at God's sovereign decree of election we next must consider the greatest question which the gospel brings before us: How can God, who is absolutely and uncompromisingly holy, pour out such blessings upon unholy sinners? How can a righteous God justify ungodly people? How can those who are deservedly on their way to hell be allowed to enter heaven? This brings us to the cross of Christ.

LIMITED ATONEMENT

Chosen sinners receive God's blessings 'through the redemption that is in Christ Jesus'.[15] The justice and holiness of God mean that our sins deserve the penalty of death. This penalty was paid in full when the Lord Jesus died at Calvary in the sinner's place; according to the apostle John, Christ 'is the propitiation for our sins'.[16] The apostle Paul also tells us that Christ 'loved the church and gave himself up for her'.[17] That Christ's death was intended specifically to save God's chosen people can be established from Scripture in many ways.

[15] *Rom.* 3:24.   [16] *1 John* 2:2.   [17] *Eph.* 5:25.

Jesus described himself as 'the good shepherd'. He then went on to say: 'I know my sheep and my sheep know me – just as the Father knows me and I know the Father – and I lay down my life for the sheep. I have other sheep that are not of this sheep pen. I must bring them also. They too will listen to my voice.'[18] It is for those who are his sheep that the good shepherd lays down his life. His sheep are described as those who listen to his voice. Christ died purposefully to save them.

Again, the same point can be drawn out from the rhetorical question posed by the apostle Paul to the Roman Christians: 'He who did not spare his own Son, but gave him up for us all – how will he not also, along with him, graciously give us all things?'[19] The implication of what Paul says here is, that no one for whom Jesus died can possibly fail to receive all that they need to reach heaven – which obviously includes faith and eternal life. These are part and parcel of the good things God grants to his people. If he was to withhold them from any for whom Christ died then Paul's rhetoric is meaningless. Therefore, we are to understand that Christ's death was intended to save the elect only; it did not atone for the sins of those who are lost.

The death of Jesus was for those whom God has chosen – those to whom he gives grace to believe in Jesus. In this special sense Christ's atoning death is spoken of as a 'limited' atonement – its saving benefits extend to a great, but nevertheless limited, number of sinners. What we need to grasp at this stage, however, is that limited atonement means a *definite* atonement. It means that through the all-sufficient death of Jesus the sin of every believer is blotted out once and for all. This has taken place not in a notional or potential sense, but really, truly, and historically.

In a ceremony that took place on the Day of Atonement in Old Testament times we can see in a vivid picture a wonderful aspect of the atoning work of Christ. On this day, Israel's high priest took two goats and by lot chose one of them to be the scapegoat. Next

[18] *John* 10:14–16.   [19] *Rom.* 8:32.

he sacrificed the other goat as a sin offering. Then he laid his hands upon the head of the scapegoat before confessing the sins of his people. This was a symbolic act signifying the transference of sin from the people to the scapegoat. The scapegoat was then led away to a lonely spot in the wilderness, never to be seen again. Just so, there was not some vague transference of sin to Christ; rather all the sin of all his people was counted as his, and, as his people's substitute, he suffered the penalty due to their sin. Having paid the price for his people's sin, he removed it from them. They would never see it again. This is why the believer in Jesus can sing with joy:

> My sin, O the bliss of this glorious thought!
> My sin, not in part but the whole,
> Is nailed to his cross and I bear it no more,
> Praise the Lord, praise the Lord, O my soul!

Jesus did not die to make salvation possible and then leave it up to us to add the crucial piece of the jigsaw by our own believing or repenting or whatever. In fact at Calvary Jesus purchased all that is necessary to secure our salvation, including the faith to receive it. The task is complete, the mission accomplished. On the cross Jesus actually secured the salvation of all his chosen ones, when he cried with a loud voice, 'It is finished!'

Now this truth is of enormous encouragement to sinners in at least four ways.

First, this truth of limited atonement is good news because it means that *all who believe in Jesus are definitely saved.* Oh, how good it is to know that Christ actually paid our debt of sin! Since God is 'faithful and just' he cannot, and will not, ask for that payment to be made a second time. It is impossible that Christ should die for a person's sin and then for that person to suffer sin's punishment again in hell. Man may be capable of such a miscarriage of justice, but with God such a thing is impossible. He is just and always acts justly. Augustus Toplady captured this note of certainty so well when he wrote:

> Since Thou hast my discharge procured,
> And freely in my room endured
> The whole of wrath divine;
> Payment God cannot twice demand,
> First from my bleeding Surety's hand,
> And then again from mine.

This is why we can offer to sinners a certain and sure salvation. The Christian gospel does not proclaim a 'maybe' or offer an uncertainty. Since Jesus has definitely secured salvation for all who trust in him, the sinner steps from condemnation to pardon, from death to life, from hell to heaven, the very moment he receives and rests by faith upon Christ alone. Surely this is wonderful news for sinners!

Secondly, the truth of limited atonement *sounds the death-knell of all religious legalism and spiritual bondage.* Many unbelievers see the life of a Christian as some kind of joyless drudgery – a kind of life in a straitjacket, fulfilling the church's expectations with the threat of hell hanging over their heads for non-compliance or for failing to add that last piece of the jigsaw of salvation, which they themselves must supply. Legalistic religion is indeed like that. It places on us the heavy burden of responsibility to get everything just right. It insists that we are obliged to fulfil certain duties in order to be saved. But such a message leaves us in fear and uncertainty, never sure if we have done all that is required or performed it perfectly. It is indeed a miserable life. But limited atonement declares the good news that at Calvary Jesus purchased our salvation by paying the price in full. Everything necessary to save us he has done already. We need add nothing more to merit our eternal acceptance. This is a truth which brings freedom and joy. The definite nature of Christ's atoning work at Calvary allows us to offer people wonderful grace, not a dead and burdensome religion.

Thirdly, the truth of limited atonement communicates the good news of God's love to the individual person. Since the Lord Jesus died for his own people particularly, the apostle Paul was able to say, 'The Son of God loved *me* and gave himself for *me.*'[20] Christ's death was designed to redeem not an amorphous mass of humanity in some general way, but his own people individually. Therefore, as we preach Christ to sinners, we can tell them of a Saviour who is able to cope with all of their own peculiar sins and miseries and needs. All that makes them feel that they are a special case, and all of which they feel particularly ashamed, presents no difficulty to a Saviour like Jesus. Some hesitate in coming to Christ because they say, 'But you don't understand. You don't really know me. I am different from other people.' They see themselves as those who are in some particular way excluded from grace. But this doctrine, (sometimes also referred to as 'particular redemption') enables us to say to all that no matter how different they feel themselves to be from others, when they believe in Christ they will find that his cross is more than a match for all their peculiar needs. What a sense of relief floods the soul when this truth is grasped for the first time!

Fourthly, the truth of limited atonement *brings great assurance.* It tells the Christian, 'You are not your own; you were bought at a price.'[21] Some delay and dither about coming to Christ because they are worried that though they may start the Christian life well, they might fall away at some time in the future. But this fear is countered by the knowledge that by his death Christ purchased men and women for God. Now since God has paid a very costly price in order to bring each of his children to himself, is it possible that he will be so careless as to lose any of them? No, instead God will take great care of each and every person whom he has redeemed with the precious blood of his own dear Son. Therefore, we are both safe and secure when we take refuge in Jesus. It is good news.

According to Charles Spurgeon, the nineteenth-century Baptist preacher, the term 'limited atonement' should not be seen as something that casts a negative light on the glory of Christ's death. On the contrary, an atonement that infallibly guarantees the salvation of real and particular sinners is the only atonement worthy of the name. In

---

[20] *Gal.* 2:20.   [21] *1 Cor.* 6:19–20.

an evangelistic sermon preached on Sunday morning, 28 February 1858, at the Music Hall, Royal Surrey Gardens, London, he said:

> We are often told that we limit the atonement of Christ, because we say that Christ has not made a satisfaction for all men, or all men would be saved. Now, our reply to this is, that, on the other hand, our opponents limit it: we do not. The Arminians say, Christ died for all men. Ask them what they mean by it. Did Christ die so as to secure the salvation of all men? They say, 'No, certainly not.' We ask them the next question – Did Christ die so as to secure the salvation of any man in particular? They answer 'No.' They are obliged to admit this if they are consistent. They say 'No, Christ has died that any man may be saved if' – and then follow certain conditions of salvation. We say, then, we will just go back to the old statement – Christ did not die so as beyond a doubt to secure the salvation of anybody, did he? You must say 'No'; you are obliged to say so, for you believe that even after a man has been pardoned, he may yet fall from grace, and perish. Now, who is it that limits the death of Christ? Why, you. You say that Christ did not die so as to infallibly secure the salvation of anybody. We beg your pardon, when you say we limit Christ's death; we say, 'No, my dear sir, it is you that do it.' We say Christ so died that he infallibly secured the salvation of a multitude that no man can number, who through Christ's death not only may be saved, but are saved, must be saved, and cannot by any possibility run the hazard of being anything but saved. You are welcome to your atonement; you may keep it. We will never renounce ours for the sake of it.

Then Spurgeon draws a lovely picture of two very different kinds of bridges in order to illustrate the difference between these two opposing views of the atonement:

> General atonement is like a great wide bridge with only half an arch; it does not go across the stream: it only professes to

go half way, it does not secure the salvation of anybody. Now, I had rather put my foot upon a [narrow] bridge . . . which went all the way across, than on a bridge that was as wide as the world, if it did not go all the way across the stream.[22]

In other words, Christ takes every sinner who trusts in him, all the way across the great chasm of sin and lands them safely on the other, heavenly, side. How vital it is for us to understand this and to remember that saving faith is all about trusting a Person (*believe in the Lord Jesus Christ*) and not a Proposition (*believe that Christ died for you*) spoken to men and women. Listen to Spurgeon, who so very helpfully draws out this important distinction.

Do not say, 'I believe that Jesus Christ died for me', and because of that feel that you are saved. I pray you to remember that the genuine faith that saves the soul has for its main element – trust – absolute rest of the whole soul – on the Lord Jesus Christ to save me, whether he died in particular or in special to save me or not, and relying, as I am, wholly and alone on him, I am saved. Afterwards I come to perceive that I have a special interest in the Saviour's blood; but if I think I have perceived that, before I have believed in Christ, then I have inverted the scriptural order of things, and I have taken as a fruit of my faith that which is only to be obtained, by rights, by the man who absolutely trusts in Christ, and Christ alone, to save.[23]

Let us also remember that while the atoning death of Christ was intended for the salvation of God's elect, its intrinsic merit is beyond all value and worth. As Spurgeon joyfully explained:

In Christ's finished work I find an ocean of merit . . . There must be sufficient efficacy in the blood of Christ, if God had so willed it, to have saved not only all in this world, but all in ten thousand worlds, had they transgressed their Maker's law. [24]

[22] *New Park Street Pulpit*, vol. 4, pp. 70–1.
[23] *Metropolitan Tabernacle Pulpit*, vol. 58, pp. 584.
[24] C. H. Spurgeon, *The Early Years* p. 171.

To know that by his death Jesus redeemed a multitude which no man can number, has been a great source of encouragement to some of the greatest evangelists and missionaries the church has ever known. It has given them strength to do the work to which God called them, and to do it well. Then let us too embrace this wonderful aspect of gospel truth. Let us walk in the footsteps of Whitefield, Brainerd, Edwards, Carey, Spurgeon, and their like, and rejoice in the glorious certainty of an atonement that saves all for whom it was designed – that is, all those who will receive and rest upon Christ alone for salvation, as he is freely offered to them in the gospel.

IRRESISTIBLE GRACE

It is by or through faith that we receive the benefits of the saving work of Jesus Christ. The great call of the gospel to all is, 'Believe in the Lord Jesus, and you will be saved.'[25] Men and women must be challenged to comply with God's call to turn from sin and trust Jesus Christ as Lord and Saviour. There should be no doubt that, according to the Bible, the responsibility to repent and believe lies with the sinner. Non-compliance with God's call in the gospel is a great sin.

Christians sometimes come across people who sincerely say, 'Yes, I see it all. I would love to believe. I wish I could believe. But I just can't.' On occasions they may have legitimate intellectual questions that need to be addressed. For example, they may need to be shown why the Christian gospel is the truth. However, though an intellectual doubt may be the apparent difficulty, their true problem actually lies much deeper than the intellect. It can be traced back to what we discovered when we considered the doctrine of total depravity. Without God's grace we are spiritually dead, and quite incapable of complying with the gospel's call.

However, the good news of the gospel is that God brings 'dead' people to spiritual life. 'But because of his great love for us, God,

[25] *Acts* 16:31.

who is rich in mercy, made us alive with Christ even when we were dead in transgressions – it is by grace you have been saved.'[26] In Christ, God has secured and provided spiritual life for his people, together with the response to the gospel which he requires. In other words, God's grace works in such a way as to guarantee the required response to the gospel's call. Later in his letter to the Ephesians, Paul further explains this with respect to our believing in Jesus: 'For it is by grace you have been saved, through faith – and this not from yourselves, it is the gift of God – not by works so that no one can boast.'[27] This is the truth of irresistible grace.

As the Holy Spirit begins to work in our hearts we often put up some form of resistance. This is only to be expected: after all, God is saving those who by nature are against him, and there is bound to be a fight and a struggle. Within every sinner there is a strong antipathy to the holiness of God and the powerful attraction of sin holds him or her back from becoming a disciple of Christ. But though there may be resistance, the grace of God proves irresistible ultimately. The Holy Spirit overcomes all our opposition. The apostle Paul himself could remember how he had resisted Christ. Telling the story of his conversion he recalled how the risen Christ appeared to him on the road to Damascus and said to him, 'Saul, Saul, why do you persecute me? It is hard for you to kick against the goads.'[28] In his pre-conversion days, the apostle had resisted Christ by persecuting Christ's followers, throwing them into jail and assenting to their deaths. But like a herdsman goading an ox, the Lord was goading him towards the foreordained day of his conversion.[29] In persecuting the church the unconverted man was kicking against the goads. But in the end the Lord Jesus revealed his grace to Paul in such a way as to bring all resistance to an end. Bowing the knee to the Lordship of Jesus Christ, 'the chief of sinners' was soon to discover that God had in fact chosen him and brought him to faith. This was irresistible grace indeed.

[26] *Eph.* 2:4-5.   [27] *Eph.* 2:8-9.
[28] *Acts* 26:14.   [29] *Gal.* 1:15.

22

Now this doctrine is of enormous help and encouragement *to those who say in sincerity, 'I would love to have your faith – but I just can't believe.'* Irresistible grace says to such, 'You feel powerless to believe. But faith does not come from within you. It is the gift of God.' They feel unable to believe and bereft of the power to manufacture faith in their hearts. But God can give them faith. Therefore, encourage them to go to God and to ask him to help them. To be without faith is to be spiritually dead, but God gives life to the dead. There is hope for them.

Indeed, if their desire for faith is sincere, that in itself is a sure sign that God is at work in them already. Let them go to God with the assurance that he will bring them through to a clear trust in the Saviour. A sincere desire for faith is the beginning of faith. Give them the words of Scripture to use in prayer, Lord 'I do believe; help me overcome my unbelief.'[30]

This doctrine of irresistible grace is also good news for others *who may stumble over the command to repent.* The gospel requires a faith that goes hand in hand with repentance. Paul taught that we 'must turn to God in repentance and have faith in our Lord Jesus'.[31]

When confronted with the challenge of turning away from a sinful lifestyle, some people wistfully respond with, 'I could never change.' They may be caught in an addictive habit or course of action. In the past they may have made strenuous efforts to turn over a new leaf or may have tried various programmes to break away from what holds them, but have failed miserably. They yearn to get out of their crushing bondage but cannot. When the call to repent comes to them, they look at their past failures and shake their heads and walk away in despair knowing that they do not have the will-power to change.

But the irresistible grace of God tells them that there is power for the powerless. Indeed, this must be the case since by nature all of us are 'dead in trespasses and sins'. Follow the logic of the great twentieth-century American theologian B. B. Warfield.

[30] *Mark* 9:24.   [31] Acts 20:21.

If the gospel is to be committed to the dead wills of sinful men and there is nothing above and beyond, who can be saved? . . . I am told to repent if I would be forgiven; but how can I repent? I only do what is wrong because I like it and I can't stop liking it or like something else better simply because I am told to do so, nor even because it is proved that it would be better for me. If I am to be changed, something must lay hold of me and change me.[32]

'And', says Paul, 'in Christ that is precisely what happens.' God makes us who were dead in transgressions and sins alive in Christ. 'For it is by grace you have been saved.' And it is not of our own effort or ability, 'so that no one can boast'. If spiritual change is the gift of God and not our own doing, then change becomes a very real prospect for us all. Whether we are naturally strong-willed or are so weak-willed by nature that any temptation easily overcomes us, is beside the point. These natural characteristics are irrelevant when it comes to irresistible grace: they are all subsumed under the category of spiritual death. But God can and does take hold of people. He raises the spiritually dead to life. He causes sinners to be born a second time. They are given spiritual life in the new birth, and this doesn't come from the flesh but from the Holy Spirit. Since this new birth is all of God and not from ourselves, no one need conclude, 'I cannot change, I can never be different.' 'All things are possible with God.'[33] Therefore they must turn from sin and trust in the Lord Jesus, looking to a merciful God to empower them as they do so.

The purpose of God's irresistible grace is not to violate the human will but to liberate it from its bondage to sin. The sinner is not saved *against* his will. Indeed, no violence is done to the will at all. Rather, the moral direction of the sinner's will is changed as the result of the new birth. The *Westminster Shorter Catechism* says that, in this work, 'convincing us of our sin and misery, enlightening our minds in the knowledge of Christ, and renewing our wills,

[32] *The Plan of Salvation*, B. B. Warfield, Eerdmans 1977, p. 49. [33] *Mark* 10:27.

he [God's Spirit] doth persuade and enable us to embrace Jesus Christ, freely offered to us in the gospel.'[34] In other words, when the Holy Spirit works in the hearts of those who hear the gospel, they find themselves longing for what they never desired before. They now want Christ. The sinner does not suddenly become an automaton that has no say in what he does, but instead finds himself wonderfully attracted to the object of his desire. Above everything else the sinner now longs for Jesus Christ and the salvation he brings. Previously the sinner was in the dark about God and sin and Christ, but now the Holy Spirit has removed the blindfold from the sinner's heart and given him spiritual eyes so that he can see these things clearly. He sees the necessity and the wisdom of gospel salvation. He sees the saving beauty and kindness of the Lord Jesus Christ; and so, by God's grace, he freely and most willingly turns to the Saviour. In the words of Philip Doddridge's hymn:

> He drew me, and I followed on,
> Charmed to confess the voice divine.

In Mark's Gospel we are given the account of how Jesus healed a man with a withered hand. Christ's command to him was, 'Stretch out your hand.'[35] But this is the very thing a person with a withered hand cannot do: the muscles have atrophied. Yet the man found that the divine command brought with it the power to obey, and his withered hand was restored. Just so, the call of Jesus comes to us to repent and believe the gospel and God's irresistible grace enables us to obey.

Here is the heart-warming answer to all those who have become so cynical about themselves that they think they could never believe and never change. 'Yes, if left to yourself that is true', we can say; 'but God has all power and God is gracious. Go to him and ask him to change you.'

We have used this truth to encourage sinners who feel their spiritual poverty. But of course, there are sinners of a different hue. There is a hardness and arrogance about them with respect to God's

---

[34] *Westminster Shorter Catechism*, Q & A 31.   [35] *Mark* 3:5.

call. Determined to continue in sin they use their inability as an excuse for not coming to Christ. 'You call on me to change but I can't change', they say. Such people must be challenged.

Imagine someone who owes a large debt, but through their own profligacy they have spent all their money and no longer have the means to pay. The fact that they have impoverished themselves does not in any way absolve them of their moral responsibility to pay. Just so, though sinners have lost the ability to turn to God, yet they are still responsible to do so. But now further imagine a great benefactor, who, knowing the profligate's inability to pay, offers them a free gift with which they can settle all their debts. Would not a refusal to take up this offer and settle their debts make their position worthy of a double condemnation? Likewise, instead of diminishing the sinner's responsibility, the fact that the power of God is available to enable sinners to repent of sin and believe in Christ increases their responsibility to comply with the terms of the gospel. It is to God we owe obedience, and in the gospel God himself is the great benefactor who makes available the power to comply. Inability was never an excuse, but when the power of God to save is made available, it is certainly no excuse. Sinners ought to come to Christ!

In this way the doctrine of irresistible grace has a dual purpose in gospel preaching. It brings comfort to those who feel their spiritual bankruptcy and it serves as a stern rebuke to the defiant.

PERSEVERANCE OF THE CHRISTIAN

There is another fear that troubles many people when they hear the message of eternal life and forgiveness in the gospel of Jesus Christ. They hear Jesus saying, 'Come, follow me', but they then think to themselves: 'I am afraid to become a Christian because I don't think I could keep it up.'

They understand that Christ is calling them to a holy life. They are aware that a Christian stands apart from the world and may experience opposition and rejection at the hands of the ungodly.

They may even know that the devil and the spiritual forces of evil will be ranged against the Christian. And with these things in mind they fear that, in spite of their initial good intentions, the effort involved in being a Christian will be too much for them in the end. They will not be able to be faithful to Christ. 'What is the point of starting out as a Christian if one can't complete the course?' And so they refuse to repent and believe in Christ.

But this is just where the fifth point of Calvinism becomes so helpful and encouraging to those on the threshold of faith. Its message is that *those who trust in Christ will be kept in Christ.* When a sinner takes hold of Christ by faith, God takes hold of him and will never let him go. This doctrine teaches that those who are truly converted to Christ will most certainly be saved.

However, we are not to imagine that this will happen regardless of how they live. The Bible does not teach that we can make a shallow choice for Christ, enter our names on a decision card, and then assume that we are eternally saved even if we let sin dominate our lives. The new birth must not be left out of the equation. All whom God forgives he also regenerates and sanctifies. The Holy Spirit takes up residence within those who trust in Christ and the power of God will keep them trusting and following the Lord Jesus.

This, however, does not imply that the Christian will be free from struggles and falls and setbacks. (God has his own wise purposes for ensuring that it is through much tribulation that his people enter his kingdom.) But it does mean that God will preserve us from ever finally turning away from Christ and will enable us to persevere in faith to the end.

Paul refers to this perseverance in Ephesians chapter 2. 'For it is by grace you have been saved, through faith – and this not from yourselves, it is the gift of God – not by works so that no one can boast. For we are God's workmanship, created in Christ Jesus to do good works, which God prepared in advance for us to do.'[36]

[36] *Eph*. 2:8–10.

Our faith in Christ is the gift of God to us. We ought to be very glad that it is not of ourselves, for if that were the case, our faith might indeed be crushed by this evil world and all that the devil throws at us in it. But our faith is a gift from God. It is therefore a faith that is sustained by his divine resources. This is how he enables us to endure hardships and persevere in faith. In the Lord's care and keeping we are able to fulfil the plan he has for us and perform those good works which he has prepared in advance for us to do.

And these verses underline *the greatness of the change* that takes place in us when we become Christians. Earlier in the chapter Paul described the Ephesians in their unconverted state as 'objects of wrath'.[37] Now in Christ they have become 'God's workmanship'[38] – 'God's works of art'! We have been rescued from the rubbish tip of this world and shall be transformed into trophies of grace by God's skilful hands. The Lord is still working on us and shaping us until finally the image of Christ is perfectly seen in every saved sinner. This is his purpose for us and he is certainly never going to give up on it or throw us away. He will preserve us until his work is completed.

And God does this *in grace*. He preserves Christian people when we are still very far from perfect. God meets us in our doubts and fears and gives us the strength to 'keep on keeping on'.

Listen to Martin Luther:

> It is the sweetest mercy of God that it is not imaginary sinners he saves but real sinners. He upholds us in our sins and accepts our work and life, worthy as these are of total rejection. He goes on doing it until he perfects and consummates us . . . We escape his condemnation because of his mercy, not because of our righteousness . . . Grace is given to heal the sick not to decorate spiritual heroes.[39]

---

[37] Eph. 2:3.   [38] Eph. 2:10.
[39] *Luther's Works* (Philadelphia: Fortress Press, 1972), vol. 31, pp. 63–4.

Or again listen to the equally comforting words of J. C. Ryle as he reflects on the truth that being counted right with God does not depend in any way on the Christian's successes or failures in life:

Many appear to forget that we are saved and justified as sinners, and only as sinners; and that we can never attain to anything higher, if we live to the age of Methuselah. *Redeemed* sinners, *justified* sinners, and *renewed* sinners doubtless we must be, – but sinners, sinners, sinners, always to the very last. They do not seem to comprehend that there is a wide difference between our justification and our sanctification. Our justification is a perfect finished work, and admits of no degrees. Our sanctification is imperfect and incomplete, and will be till the last hour of our life.[40]

With this assurance we can rejoice in Christ despite our failures and enjoy our Christian lives to the glory of God. We are to aim at perfection.[41] When we inevitably fall short we are not to be downcast, but realize that God has us safely in his hands and is still working on us. The cross of Jesus has redeemed us once and for all. In coming to Christ we are not given temporary life, but eternal life. This life begun in the new birth is never to be forfeited. Therefore, when we invite sinners to Christ we are inviting them to a new life of joy and peace.[42] Those who believe in the doctrines of grace are not inviting people to a life of anxiety and religious bondage, which is the inevitable conclusion of believing that our following of Christ is ultimately down to our own ability and will-power. Instead, we are inviting them to a Saviour who said, 'My sheep listen to my voice; I know them, and they follow me. I give them eternal life, and they shall never perish; no one can snatch them out of my hand. My Father, who has given them to me, is greater than all; no one can snatch them out of my Father's hand. I and the Father are one.'[43] What could be greater good news than this?

[40] J. C. Ryle, *Assurance*, Evangelical Press, 1989, pp. 94–5.
[41] *2 Cor.* 13:11.　　[42] *Rom.* 15:13.　　[43] *John* 10:27-30.

CONCLUSION

In the first place, we have seen that the five points of Calvinism are *full of cogent and loving evangelistic arguments which persuade sinners to come to Christ.* They are like precious balm to the soul; by addressing man's deepest problems they heal the guilty conscience and fearful heart. For these reasons alone we ought to be unashamed of the doctrines of grace. Let us confidently and joyfully proclaim and explain them to needy sinners.

Secondly, we have also seen that the doctrines of grace are *full of pastoral encouragement and consolation, and when carefully explained will surely promote healthy Christian growth and living in our churches.* A low view of God and his grace in salvation will, more often than not, produce a weak and anaemic Christianity. How important it is that from the very beginning of the Christian life the believer is given a robust vision of God's sovereign saving work. The doctrines of grace must never be neglected in our pastoral ministry.

Warfield's words capture the vision of God and the Christian life to which the five points of Calvinism direct us.

> In Calvinism, then, objectively speaking, theism comes to its rights; subjectively speaking, the religious relation attains its purity; soteriologically speaking, evangelical religion finds at length its full expression and its secure stability. Theism comes to its rights only in a teleological conception of the universe, which perceives in the entire course of events the orderly out-working of the plan of God, who is the author, preserver and governor of all things, whose will is consequently the ultimate cause of all. The religious relation attains its purity only when an attitude of absolute dependence on God is not merely temporarily assumed in the act, say, of prayer, but is sustained through all the activities of life, intellectual, emotional, executive. And evangelical religion reaches stability only when the sinful soul rests in humble, self-emptying trust purely on

the God of grace as the immediate and sole source of all the efficiency which enters into its salvation. And these things are all the formative principles of Calvinism.[44]

These truths show God as he really is. Such a vision will lead people, as Warfield indicated, to that 'self-emptying trust' in God in every area of their lives – which is the essence of thorough and genuine Christian conversion. The doctrines of grace will give new 'babes in Christ' a good start in the Christian life.

But there is a third and even greater reason why these truths should be taught in an evangelistic setting – *the glory of God in Christ*. The doctrines of grace ascribe salvation to God alone. The extent to which we skirt around or skip over them, is the extent to which we deny God his rightful glory. Salvation is of the Lord and all of grace. Let us never rob the Lord of what rightfully belongs to him.

The doctrines of grace bring encouragement to the sinner, stability to the Christian, and glory to God.

'So do not be ashamed', says Paul, 'But join with me in suffering for the gospel, by the power of God, who saved us and called us to a holy life – not because of anything we have done but because of his own purpose and grace. This grace was given us in Christ Jesus before the beginning of time, but it has now been revealed through the appearing of our Saviour, Christ Jesus, who has destroyed death and has brought life and immortality to light through the gospel.'[45]

Commenting on these verses, John Calvin said, 'If the gospel is not preached, it is as if Jesus Christ were buried – out of sight. Let us, therefore, do him the honour (since we see all the world so far out of the way) of holding firmly to this wholesome doctrine.'[46]

---

[44] B. B. Warfield, 'Calvinism', in *Works of Benjamin B. Warfield*, vol. 5, p. 355, repr. Baker, 1981.

[45] 2 *Tim*. 1:8-10.

[46] *Grace and Its Fruits: Selections from John Calvin on the Pastoral Epistles*, Evangelical Press, 2000, p. 104.

By the same author:

COMING TO FAITH IN CHRIST

A straightforward summary of the gospel for those who may be considering the Christian faith for the first time.

ISBN 0 85151 252 6, 16 pp., booklet.

With John Peet:

GOD'S RICHES

A Workbook on the Doctrines of Grace

Serves as an introductory workbook to Christian doctrine; leads the student through the biblical teaching on God and his character, works, and sovereignty, man and his sin, redemption in Christ, and the way of grace.

ISBN 0 85151601 7, 96 pp., large pbk.

For free illustrated catalogue please write to
THE BANNER OF TRUTH TRUST

3 Murrayfield Road,
Edinburgh EH12 6EL
UK

P O Box 621, Carlisle,
Philadelphia 17013,
USA

www.banneroftruth.co.uk